Sampson's First Christmas

*A Children's
Church Pageant*

Carlene Morton

CSS Publishing Company, Inc., Lima, Ohio

To the Hawfields Presbyterian Church
congregation for their
support, encouragement, and love

For more information about CSS Publishing Company resources, visit our website at www.csspub.com or email us at custserv@csspub.com or call (800) 241-4056.

Cover design by Barbara Spencer
ISBN-13: 978-0-7880-2406-1
ISBN-10: 0-7880-2406-X

PRINTED IN U.S.A.

Production Notes

Cast

Speaking

Ma	Felicia Frog
Pa	Baby Frog
Sampson Squirrel	Bertha Bunny
Baby Squirrel	Oliver Owl
Cat	Millie Mouse
Snooper Dog	Choir

Nonspeaking

Little Squirrels (any number)
Little Bunnies (any nuumber)

Costumes

Pa wears a flannel shirt, bibbed overalls, and boots.

Ma wears an old housedress and shawl.

Patterns for the animal hats are included. Use colored craft foam with adhesive backing (available at craft stores).

Colors needed:

Brown for dog
Green for frogs
Black for cat
Gray for squirrels
Brown for owl
Gray for mouse
Black, white, and gray for bunnies
White for eyes
Pink for bunny noses and animal ears
Black/Brown for whiskers and noses
Orange for beak

One 9" x 12" sheet of adhesive foam is needed for each face. The number of sheets required depends upon number of actors chosen to be used in play. The size of the animal families may be adapted to fit the number of children who wish to participate.

Directions For Hats

1. Remove pullout section of animal face patterns and make copies.
2. Cut out face pattern with ears and trace onto foam. Cut out foam.
3. Cut out nose pattern and trace onto foam. Cut out foam and remove backing. Attach nose to face.
4. Cut out whites of eyes pattern and trace onto foam. Cut out foam and remove backing. Attach whites of eyes to face.
5. Cut out pupils of eyes pattern and trace onto foam. Cut out foam and remove backing. Attach pupils to eyes on face.
6. Cut out inner ears pattern and trace onto pink foam. Cut out foam and remove backing. Attach inner ears to outer ears.
7. Cut out other small piece patterns (whiskers, frog markings, owl's beak, and others) and trace onto foam. Cut out foam and attach to face. (Whiskers and other markings may be made with black permanent magic marker.)
8. Choose baseball hats that match the color of the faces. However, any colored hat will suffice. Pull backing away from only the face parts that will touch the baseball hat. Cut this backing away. Leave backing on foam that will not touch hat. Attach face to hat.
9. Actors wear colored sweat shirts and sweat pants that match the color of the face of his/her character. Actors may prefer to wear tights that match their hats.

Other accessories may be added to the costumes. The cat and mouse costumes may include long tails made from socks sewn together, stuffed, and sewn onto pants. The squirrel costume may include a big, bushy tail made from furry material and sewn onto pants. The bunnies may wear bunny bedroom shoes and tails attached to their sweat pants made from cotton balls.

Suggestions

To avoid a noisy backstage, actors sit with their animal families in various locations on stage.

Animal hats (directions included) help prevent distractions for young actors.

The animal patterns may be transferred to poster board, colored, and the eyes cut away. Attach the poster board to dowels and use them as masks for the play.

The patterns may be attached to poster board and then to dowels to be used as puppets. If the play is performed with stick puppets, actors can portray Ma and Pa. These two characters sit in front of the puppet stage for Act 1 and interact with the puppets during Act 5.

Scenery

Potted plants and artificial trees are placed on stage creating a forest atmosphere.

A Christmas tree trimmed with ornaments made from food (directions included) sits up stage in the center.

The backdrop is made from blue shower curtains on which tree trunks of varying widths are drawn. Use brown and black permanent markers to color the tree trunks. Green and brown grass complete the backdrop.

Props

A "log" will be needed for the characters to use for seating, either real or a block of wood painted to look like a log.

The Christmas tree is decorated with ornaments made from food suitable for animals. Families are invited to participate in a nature walk to gather pine cones, pecans, and acorns for some of the decorations in the weeks before the play. A tree-trimming party offers an opportunity for family fellowship. Refreshments (for human consumption) will be a treat. Families of the actors can be a part of the play. When Ma and Pa take Sampson to hear the church choir during the play, families can stand in the audience and sing "Joy To The World." The tree-trimming party also provides a chance to ask families to participate in the play's choir and to practice the song.

Christmas Tree Decorations

Pine cones are smeared with peanut butter and rolled in bird seed. A red bow is tied onto the pine cone with a loop suitable for hanging.

Red bows are tied onto dog biscuits.

Red bows are attached to apples.

Adults may use hot glue to make pecan and acorn ornaments. Six nuts of a kind are hot glued together and a bow is attached for hanging.

Popcorn and cranberries are strung on lightweight fishing line.

After the families decorate the tree, it can be placed in the church vestibule or the fellowship hall with a sign advertising the date and time of the play. After the production, place the tree in the churchyard for all to enjoy.

Sampson's First Christmas

(Ma and Pa walk down the aisle and sit on the log; Sampson Squirrel and other Little Squirrels stick their heads out so that audience sees them eavesdropping.)

Ma: Hurry up, Pa, quit your dawdling. We have to get home and start cooking Christmas dinner. We should not have stayed so long at Junior and Sissy Sue's house.

Pa: I know, but I need to rest a while. I am not the young whipper-snapper I used to be. It is a fer piece from Junior's.

Ma: We will rest a few minutes. But I can hardly wait to smell that sweet smell of Christmas cooking. Mm-mm-mm.

Pa: I know what ya mean, Ma. I kind of like the taste of Christmas, too. *(pats stomach)* Sissy Sue sure did have some mighty fine Christmas goodies.

Ma: She was lucky to have fixed so much. She had just enough for those Christmas carolers. And their Christmas sounds sure put a tingle in my ears and heart.

Pa: Yes, and Sissy Sue's house had a beautiful Christmas look. I just love the pretty sights of Christmas.

Ma: Me, too. The Christmas season makes me feel so good, so happy. You rested enough Pa? We need to get home.

(Ma and Pa exit. Squirrels enter)

Sampson: Oh! Oh! What is this thing they call Christmas?

Baby Squirrel: I don't know. But we need to find out.

Sampson: It sounds wonderful. You go home and tell Mom that I will be there as soon as I find Christmas.

(Baby squirrel exits; Cat walks across stage meowing)

Act 2

Sampson: Let me see. Where do I begin? I know I will call my friend with the good nose. Snooper! Snooper!

(Snooper Dog enters)

Sampson: Help me.

Snooper: *(talks slowly and through nose)* What do you need, Sampson? Do not keep me too long. I am following the scent of a cat. Have you seen one go by?

Sampson: No, but have you smelled Christmas? Ma and Pa say it smells sweet.

Snooper: What is Christmas?

Sampson: That is what I am asking you.

Snooper: Well, if Christmas smells sweet then it must be ... *(finger on chin thinking)* like a big steak bone, or ... like the bark on an old oak tree.

Sampson: Those things do not smell sweet.

Snooper: *(sniffing)* Not as sweet as that cat I smell. He must have gone this way. See ya, Sampson! *(Snooper exits)*

Act 3

Sampson: Maybe it will be better to search for the taste of Christmas.

(Felicia and Baby Frog begin to ribbit off stage)

Sampson: Felicia, is that you?

(Felicia and Baby Frog hop on stage)

Felicia: Sampson, why do you look so sad?

Sampson: I am trying to find out about Christmas and my friend Snooper knows nothing about it. Help me.

Felicia: I will try. Tell me more.

Sampson: Pa said he liked the taste of Christmas. Have you ever tasted Christmas?

Felicia: What is Christmas?

Sampson: That is what I am asking you.

Felicia: If Christmas is a good taste, it must be ... like the taste of that big, juicy, black fly I had this morning for breakfast.

Sampson: Oh, yuck!

Felicia: Or, it could be the taste of a family of crickets on a summer night. Kneedeep, kneedeep.

Sampson: That sounds like a frog choking on a cricket.

Baby Frog: Mama, Mama I just heard a fly go by.

Felicia: Which way did it go? That is our dinner.

Baby Frog: Come this way. I will show you.

Felicia: Bye, Sampson. Good luck on your Christmas hunt.

(Felicia and Baby Frog exit)

Sampson: It is no use. I am never going to find out what Christmas is.

Act 4

Sampson: I know, I will call Bertha Bunny. She has the biggest ears in the forest. I bet she will know what Christmas is and where to find it. Bertha! Bertha!

(Bertha and Little Bunnies enter)

Sampson: *(talking fast)* Bertha I need your help. I have got to find it. Do you know where it is?

(Little Bunnies hop around stage)

Bertha: *(with a southern accent, slower and drawn out)* Children, sit still. *(Little Bunnies sit)* Sampson, what are you so excited about? Slow down now and tell Ol' Bertha.

Sampson: Bertha, I heard Ma and Pa talking about something called Christmas and how the happy sound of Christmas put a tingle in their hearts and ears. What does Christmas sound like?

Bertha: What is Christmas?

Sampson: That is what I am asking you.

Bertha: If Christmas sounds good, then it must be ... the sound of me chewing on a crispy carrot. Yes, that is about the sweetest sound I know.

Sampson: I do not think so. You are no help at all.

Bertha: It could be the sound of crispy lettuce popping out of the spring earth. Or, maybe it's the sound of my cute little feet scampering through the woods.

Sampson: Thanks for all of your help. Just go, and do not forget your children.

(Bertha and Little Bunnies exit)

Act 5

Sampson: Maybe I will ask someone about the sights of Christmas. There is no one who sees better than Oliver the Owl. And he is so smart. Oliver!

Oliver: Whooo is calling me?

Sampson: It is me, Sampson. Help me. Have you seen Christmas? Ma and Pa say it is pretty.

Oliver: What is Christmas?

Sampson: That is what I am asking you.

Oliver: If Christmas is pretty, then it must be ...

Sampson: What? Tell me.

Oliver: It must be a full, white moon.

Sampson: I do not think that is Christmas.

Oliver: It could be little mice running through the leaves. Whooo knows?

(Oliver exits)

Act 6

(Millie Mouse enters)

Millie: Why the sad face?

Sampson: I have been trying to find out what Christmas is. I know it smells sweet, it tastes wonderful, it sounds cheerful, it looks pretty, and it makes you feel good. None of my friends have been able to help me. Do you have any ideas?

Millie: Maybe it could be a piece of cheese about the size of a watermelon. Yes, that would certainly smell sweet. My teeth biting into it would taste ever so wonderful and the sound would be cheerful. A piece of cheese that big would be pretty. And — ahh — it would make me feel so good.

Sampson: Maybe a big piece of cheese would be good for you but it does not do anything for me.

Millie: Well, excuse me. *(wanders off mumbling about different kinds of cheese)* American, Swiss, Bleu, Cheddar, any old kind will do.

Sampson: *(crying)* I wish I could find Christmas.

Act 7

(Ma and Pa enter; Sampson tries to hide)

Ma: Little squirrel, whatever is the matter? Do not be frightened. We love squirrels. Come closer so that we can hear you.

Sampson: I heard you talking on your way home from Junior and Sissy Sue's house. I want to know what Christmas is.

Pa: Follow us.

(Ma and Pa walk over to the Choir, Sampson follows)

(Choir sings the first chorus of "Joy To The World," then they quietly hum the tune, fading to silence)

Sampson: What is that?

Ma: That is the church choir.

Sampson: What are they singing about?

Pa: They are singing about God sending his Son, Jesus, to save all of the people in the world.

Ma: Christmas is a day. It is the day Jesus was born.

Sampson: It is Jesus' birthday?

Ma and Pa: Yes.

Sampson: So Christmas is like a big birthday party?

Ma and Pa: Yes!

Sampson: Where is Jesus?

Pa: He is right here. *(puts hand over his heart)*

Ma: He is in our hearts.

Sampson: What is the smell of Christmas?

Ma: The smells of food, apples, and trees. The smells that remind us of Christmases in the past and Christmases yet to be.

Sampson: And the taste of Christmas?

Ma: It is the joy of cooking and sharing all kinds of good foods with family and friends.

Sampson: Is the sound of Christmas what we heard the people singing earlier?

Pa: Yes, and bells jingling and a jolly Ho! Ho! Ho!

Sampson: Can you see Christmas?

Pa: Certainly — all around you. Candles, lights, presents.

Sampson: I think I am beginning to understand what Christmas feels like.

Ma: Call all of your forest friends. Pa and I have a little Christmas for you in our backyard.

Sampson: Millie, Felicia, Snooper, Bertha, Oliver come here.

(All characters, including little ones, enter and stand around Christmas tree)

All: Ooh, aah.

Sampson: The tree is decorated with food for us.

All: It is Christmas. It is Christmas.

Snooper: It's beginning to smell.

Felicia: It's beginning to taste.

Bertha: It's beginning to sound.

Oliver: It's beginning to look.

(Everyone sings to the tune of the last verse of "It's Beginning To Look a Lot Like Christmas")

All: It's beginning to feel a lot like Christmas
Everywhere we go.
Every day we start
With Jesus in our heart.
And we hope you will, too!
Merry Christmas, Everyone!